SOUTH AFRICA

AN AERIAL CLOSE UP

Acknowledgements
**The publishers wish to thank the following for their invaluable
assistance in the production of this book:**
British Airways
Motswari – M'bali Game Lodges
South African Tourism Board (Head Office, Pretoria)
South African Tourism Board (London Office)
South African Defence Force (Dept. of Public Relations)
Southern Sun and Holiday Inns of South Africa
The University of Pretoria Mammal Research Institute (Mr. P.B. Best)
Tropair (Pilot Jan Viljoen)

CLB 1511
This edition published 1986 by Central News Agency Ltd.,
  Laub Street, New Centre, Johannesburg, South Africa.
© 1986 Illustrations and text: Colour Library Books Ltd.,
  Guildford, Surrey, England.
Photography by Neil Sutherland.
Co-ordination by Hanni Edmonds.
Colour separations by Llovet S.A., Barcelona, Spain.
Printed and bound in South Africa by CTP Book Printers, Cape
All rights reserved.
ISBN 0 86283 464 3

SOUTH AFRICA

AN AERIAL CLOSE UP

Introduction

Down below, the herd of elephants, several hundred strong, browse among the scrub and fever trees of Kruger Park. As they move, a cloud of yellow dust rises and drifts away in the fierce noonday heat of the Transvaal Lowveld.

This is an image of old Africa, brought forward into the present. It is only one of many such images conjured up by an aerial journey over southern Africa. From the sky we can look down on a vast natural tapestry as it unfolds. For despite the advances of man, this is still a land where the grandeur of nature overshadows the achievements of humans.

Here are a thousand dramatic scenes, painted the colours of dust, of the savannah grassland, dotted with the green of ancestral forests and touched with snow on the high mountains. Harsh and beautiful by turns, the landscape is sculpted by wind and rain, marked above all by the relentless sun of Africa, both the giver and taker of life.

Most of the country consists of a high central plateau, flanked to the south and east by mountain ranges, among them the Hottentots Hollands, the Outeniquas, and the majestic Drakensberg Range of Natal. Between the mountains and the sea is squeezed a fertile coastal 'terrace'. On the west, the land runs out in a bleak, near-desert fringe, abutting the ocean. The chill waters of the Benguela Current on the west have their counterpart in the warm Agulhas Stream of the Indian Ocean to the east.

As a separate continent, Africa was born some 180-million years ago. The huge flattened bowl of the subcontinent became separated from the land mass of 'Gondwanaland'. Since then it has seen long, temperate periods when the rest of the earth was locked in ice. For millions of years the central plateau was a marsh, where dense fern forests teemed with prehistoric life.

Then the earth became warmer and Africa became the sun-baked continent of today. The old animals died out, and new ones took their place. The lion and the elephant, springbok and impala, buffalo and kudu, roamed the dry savannah uplands. The hippo shared the mudbanks and the pools of the rivers with one of the few survivors of the reptilian past, the crocodile.

In time they were joined by a new creature, at first very much in a minority. The scattered groups of early men emerged in historic times as the Bushmen and Hottentots. They lived as hunters and herders, in harmony with the wildlife. Then began an invasion of their land from the north, with the appearance of dark-skinned Bantu-speaking Nguni peoples from central Africa. As they settled along the eastern seaboard yet another intruder arrived, this time from the sea. At the end of the 15th century, Portuguese caravels picked their way down the west coast, against the power of the Benguela Current. They were driven by dreams of a passage around Africa to the wealth of the Orient. In 1488, Bartolomé Dias rounded Cape Agulhas to become the first European to sail the Indian Ocean.

For a century and a half, the Portuguese plied their trade around the coast. But it was only in the mid-17th century that a permanent settlement was undertaken. It was the work of a small group of Dutch settlers, servants of the Dutch East India Company under their Commander, Jan Van Riebeeck. They set up a small revictualling station on the shore where the city of Cape Town now stands, in the shadow of Table Mountain.

Van Riebeeck's modest wood fort has long gone. Today, a bustling, modern metropolis sprawls around the lower slopes of Table Mountain and Devil's Peak. These in turn are part of the craggy complex of the Cape Peninsula. Once an island, it is now joined to the hinterland by the expanse of the Cape Flats. From the air it presents a splendid spectacle, a blend of land and sea, forest and mountain. Around its shores, a chain of picturesque villages overlooks some of the country's finest beaches. Not surprisingly, this is a major tourist area, with the pleasures of the present enhanced by the legacy of the past, and the memory of a more gracious age. The oak-shaded valley of Constantia, for example, saw the making of some of the country's earliest wines, the toast of European royalty in their day. It contrasts with the wind-scoured heights of the Cape Point Nature Reserve, tapering down to Cape Point itself. The wayward winds and currents which assault this promontory gave the area its first name, the 'Cabo Tormentoso', or 'Cape of Storms'.

From the Peninsula, the blue horizon of False Bay beckons eastwards. The way skirts the Hottentots-Holland mountains, following the narrow coastal terrace between mountains and sea. The terrain below is grey-green, the colour of the indigenous 'fynbos' vegetation. The smallest of the world's six floral 'kingdoms', it is nevertheless one of the most varied, showing unique adaptations to the conditions in this winter rainfall region.

It contrasts with the neat, geometric patterns of the farmlands of the south coast. Beyond Hermanus, the mountains draw back to leave a broad segment of low-lying land, long cleared for sheep and wheat-growing. In spring the wheatlands show as a vivid green, darkening to yellow-brown as the summer progresses. With the spread of agriculture, little remains of the original

landscape, though pockets of 'fynbos' and wetland ecology are preserved in the Nature Reserve at De Hoop Vlei. This is the home of over 200 of the Cape's bird species, including many coastal and migrant varieties. Nearby is the Potberg mountain, nesting ground for the few surviving families of the Cape vulture. Once hunted as a pest, it is now rigorously protected. Further inland is the beautiful Bontebok National Park, where the bontebok, another threatened species, is making a slow recovery.

If nature has been tamed on land, the sea still obeys its own laws. For this is a dangerous part of the coast, which has seen over 200 wrecks since the day when Dias first rounded Cape Agulhas. Today the most southerly tip of Africa is marked by a small, weather-beaten lighthouse. A few kilometres to the east is where, in April 1815, the British vessel *Arniston* foundered in a storm. On the beach below the village, which is now named after the ship, the bodies of over 300 men, women and children were washed up. Forty years later, there was a still more devastating wreck at what is now called Danger Point. Here, in the early hours of 26 February 1852, the British troop-carrier *Birkenhead*, carrying several hundred young recruits for the Eighth Kaffir War, struck an offshore reef. The ship broke up and sank with the loss of 445 lives.

As the Indian Ocean shore begins its slow swing northwards, the mountains rejoin the coast. This is the start of the Garden Route, heralded by the town of George. One of the most beautiful and varied areas in southern Africa, it is justly a target for holiday-makers. A series of lakes and lagoons is woven into the shore, including Rondevlei, Swartvlei and Groenvlei. Each has its own character and wildlife. At the charming town of Knysna, with its rocky Heads overlooking the ocean, is a lagoon and estuary making up one of the richest wetland areas in the country, with some 350 species of fish and invertebrates.

But the dominant image here is that of the forests. The region is the meeting point of two climate systems – of the winter rainfall area to the south and the summer rainfall area to the north. Up to 1 300mm of rain annually generates dense, brooding forests, overlooked by the Outeniqua and Kouga mountains. Here, some 40 500 hectares of indigenous trees are preserved and protected. This shadowy realm contains ancient yellowwoods of great size, as well as stinkwood, saffronwood, blackwood, and many other species. The almost impenetrable undergrowth is the home of a myriad small creatures, including indigenous birds such as the Knysna loerie, an exotic relative of the European cuckoo.

After the relative luxuriance of the coastal region, the scene beyond the rampart of the mountains makes a stark contrast. The plain of the Little Karoo is sandwiched between the Outeniquas and the Swartberg range to the north. High and dry, it stretches for about 250km from west to east, and is about 60km across. The 'capital' of the area is Oudtshoorn, a town synonymous with ostrich farming. The fashion for ostrich feathers in ladies' hats began towards the end of the last century. At the height of the boom, almost all other kinds of farming disappeared from the 'Klein Karoo', which became one vast ostrich farm, with more than 750 000 birds. Fortunes were made, and fine houses – the celebrated 'Ostrich Palaces' – were built. Alas, changing fashions and the advent of the motor car swept away the elegant plumage by the end of the First World War. The humbler use for feather dusters, however, ensures a continuing population of ostriches.

The Little Karoo is the curtain-raiser for its larger companion, the Great Karoo. It begins beyond the Swartberg Mountains, and stretches away westwards to the Atlantic fringe. The name 'Karoo' comes from the Hottentot word for 'land of thirst'. With a strange, bleak beauty of its own, the region appears at first glance to be almost barren. Long, low koppies are crowned with caps of hard dolomite and hardy vegetation seems to cling for survival to the hard, hot earth. Little rainfall occurs, with only occasional thunderstorms bringing flash floods to irrigate the land.

This arid area was once the marshland which covered two-thirds of the plateau of southern Africa. The geological structure of the landscape was laid down between 250 and 150 million years ago. It comprises three major levels. The deepest is the Dwyka series, laid down by an ancient sea. Above this is the Ecca series, the remains of a vast tropical forest. The present surface level is the Beaufort series. This, too, is rich in fossil remains. They include large numbers of dinosaurs, making the area a happy hunting ground for palaeontologists. Through these sedimentary layers, molten material from still deeper levels was extruded. This created horizontal 'sills' which form the familiar caps on the Karoo koppies.

For many years, because of the lack of water, there was little farming here. Then, in the 1880s, windmills were introduced to bring up underground water. Now the Great Karoo is the scene of large flocks of merino sheep, which thrive on the stunted but nutritious vegetation. Of the great herds of game which once roamed the land, little remains. Near the town of Graaff-Reinet is Mountain Zebra National Park, home of the last surviving members of the Cape Mountain Zebra. Near here, too, is the awesome Valley of Desolation, with its fantastic rock formations. The entire valley has been declared a National Monument, and is also the setting for the Karoo Nature Park.

Back on the coast, the horizon changes again as we approach Port Elizabeth and the old 'Settler Country'. This, too, is predominantly sheep and stock-farming country, though Port Elizabeth, on its bluff overlooking Algoa Bay, is a growing industrial centre, with a corner on the local motor vehicle manufacture.

It was in Algoa Bay, on 12 March 1488, that Bartolomé Dias reached the limit of his voyage. He erected a commemorative 'padrão' cross on the promontory now called Kwaaihoek, at the eastern end of the bay. He intended to push on still further, but the threat of mutiny from a weary crew persuaded him to turn back. The Portuguese sailors' opinion of this part of the coast was shared by many others in the coming years, including the survivors of the *Dodington*. Wrecked off

Bird Island in the bay in July 1755, the ship went down, taking with it most of the crew and the treasure of the conqueror of India, Robert Clive.

The first permanent European settlement took place in the early nineteenth century. A scheme to settle English immigrants on this part of the coast was put forward by the Governor of the Cape of Good Hope, Lord Charles Somerset. Four thousand people sailed from England in 21 transports, the first dropping anchor in Algoa Bay on 9 April 1820.

The newcomers were carried ashore, and deposited with their belongings on the beach. There they took stock of their new country. To their dismay they discovered that Africa was not the green and pleasant land of their dreams. A struggle for survival against heavy odds followed. These included their own ignorance of farming in an alien climate, and the depredations of the local Xhosas on the settlers' flocks. Once established, though, the community grew, with Port Elizabeth acting as the port for its produce. Inland, other settler towns grew up, including Cradock and Grahamstown, now a university centre of note.

Today, while most of the area is turned over to farming, there are still enclaves of old Africa. An important preserve is found in the Addo Elephant National Park. It is situated at a junction of three different systems of vegetation - the Southern Cape, the semi-arid Karoo, and the sub-tropical East African. The result is 5 000 hectares of dense, evergreen thickets and thorn brake, providing good sustenance for a herd of about 120 elephants.

'Settlers Country' shades to the north-east into the historic 'Border Country', now the Homeland of the Ciskei. The early years of settlement in this region were troubled. There were nine successive 'Kaffir Wars' with the local Xhosa tribes, spanning nearly a century. By the mid-nineteenth century, however, peace had been secured, and with it an increased prosperity. The main town here is the port of East London, at the mouth of the Buffalo River. Scenic attractions of the area include the beautiful Hogsback range, north of King William's Town.

Beyond the Kei River begin the green hills of the Transkei. Like the Ciskei, this is an independent Homeland, with its capital at Umtata. To the north, it is bounded by the Umzimkulu River. In between lie 250km of the Wild Coast. A number of tribes live in the region, including the Gcaleka Xhosas in the south and the Pondo and Mpondomise people in the north.

The Transkei marks the lower limit of the savannah grassland, where it joins the 'fynbos' kingdom of the Cape. From the air it presents a quiet, pastoral scene, dotted with brown and white mud huts and flocks of goats, the mark of a man's wealth. The rocky shore of the Wild Coast itself is spectacular. Its most famous feature is the 'Hole in the Wall' formation, near Coffee Bay. It is known locally as 'esiKhaleni', or the 'Place of the Sound', after the roaring of the sea through the hole in this colossal, detached cliff.

Like the 'Border Country', the Transkei had an embattled early history. The southward migration of the tribes made this a heavily populated area by the time the first European settlers arrived. Despite the Xhosas' advantage in numbers, the clash of the rifle and the assegai was an unequal one. By the 1850s, the power of the tribes had been broken. Their defeat was reflected in one of the most bizarre and tragic events in Xhosa history. In March 1856, a young girl named Nongquase, from the Gcaleka clan in the south, saw a vision of the tribal ancestors in a stream. The spirits promised to drive away the white men, but on condition that the people kill all their cattle and destroy their crops. For a year the ritual slaughter continued, until 18 February 1857, the day the prophesy was due to be fulfilled. Like any other day in the year, it came and went. Left in a blighted land, about 25 000 people died of starvation.

By now, we are well into the summer rainfall region. There is a hint of the tropics in the air as we cross the Umtamvuna River and fly over the south coast of Natal.

A procession of villages and holiday resorts follows the shore. The warm sea has been made safe from the menace of sharks by a system of nets. The capital of the province is the coastal city of Durban. Today it is the main cargo port in southern Africa, handling 18 million tonnes of cargo annually. From Durban, we follow the road inland, to Pietermaritzburg, once the Voortrekker capital of the region, and the wide perspectives of the Valley of a Thousand Hills. This is ancestral Zulu country, and the tribal Homeland of KwaZulu stretches away beyond the northern horizon.

From here, the coastal hills rise in echelon to the magnificent battlements of the high Drakensberg range, the 'Mountains of the Dragon'. Part of the Stormberg geological series, it is one of *the* sights of southern Africa, and a paradise for mountaineers. Here is the great amphitheatre of Mont-aux-Sources, in the Royal Natal National Park and, just beyond the border with the Orange Free State, the Golden Gate Highlands National Park, with its cave sandstone formations.

Natal has had a colourful and frequently bloodthirsty history. The presiding ghost here is that of Shaka. He was born in 1787, the illegitimate son of a young chief of the minor Zulu clan. Conscripted into the army of the paramount chief of the region, Dingiswayo, he distinguished himself in battle and rose rapidly to command. He developed the short, stabbing spear and the tactical 'horns and chest of the bull' battle formation. After Dingiswayo's death he took power, and soon unleashed his armies on the surrounding tribes. He created an empire the size of Europe, but left widespread devastation in the wake of his conquests. In 1826 he transferred his capital to Dukuza, on the site of today's quiet seaside town of Stanger. There, in September 1828, at the age of 41 he was murdered by his half-brother, the wily and treacherous Dingane.

By now the white man had begun to move into the territory. The city of Durban began life as a group of shacks on the Rio de Natal – the lagoon had been discovered by the Portuguese on Christmas Day. It was a small trading station, watched with wary tolerance by the neighbouring Zulus. While English influence predominated here, a new force appeared from the Highveld, with the first parties of Voortrekkers.

Since the British had annexed the Cape at the end of the 18th century, tension had built up between the Dutch farmers and their new rulers. In the mid-1830s, in the wake of the emancipation of their slaves by the British, the farmers had begun their Great Trek to the north. One branch of the Trek moved down through the Drakensberg into Natal, in search of land on which to settle. Dingane's answer to their overtures was to murder their leader, Piet Retief, and his companions.

The Trekkers took vengeance in the Battle of Blood River, where they decisively defeated Dingane's impis. Zulu power was far from broken, however. It saw a later resurgence under Cetswayo in the Zulu War. He challenged the might of the British Empire, inflicting a grievous defeat at the Battle of Isandhlwana. Memories abound here, too, of a later and still more bitter conflict, the Boer War. The town of Ladysmith was the scene of a protracted seige of the British garrison by the Boers. Along the Tugela River, the army of General Buller and Louis Botha's sharpshooters faced each other in a series of bloody deadlocks in the bends of the river.

The ending of the war saw a new prosperity in Natal, much of it based on the growing of sugar cane. In 1851, Edward Morewood had introduced this new crop to the region. In the 1860s, indentured labourers were imported from India to work in the fields, the Zulus being disdainful of such labour. The immigrants formed the basis for today's flourishing Indian community. Their ornate, richly decorated temples add an exotic note to the local architecture.

In the northern part of KwaZulu, the coastal terrace opens out. Industry is represented in the massive new export harbour at Richard's Bay. The main outlet for the Transvaal's coal production, it exhibits a strenuous modernity which contrasts with the nearby domain of nature. The hot, humid climate supports many subtropical plants, including lala palms and mangroves.

Five mangrove genera from three distinct families are found on this coast, dominated by the white mangrove, *Avicennia*. A further feature of the shore here is in the underwater coral reefs, habitat of many thousands of brightly coloured marine species. On land, the wildlife is protected in a number of fine parks and reserves. They include the St Lucia Game Reserve, with its massed flocks of pelicans and flamingoes, its crocodiles and hippos, the Sodwana Bay National Park, and the Kosi Bay Park, near the border with Moçambique. Here, too, is Bhanga Nek, with the nesting beaches of the loggerhead and leatherback turtles – of which the latter, the world's largest turtle, has attained a recorded length of almost three metres.

As we turn inland again to rejoin the Drakensberg mountains, a new landscape emerges. The range culminates in a northern spur which is part of the Eastern Transvaal. This rim of the Highveld plateau, the Drakensberg Escarpment, is known locally as the 'Berg'. From the air, it appears as a counterpoint of overlapping strata, ending in precipitous cliffs, girt about with thick forests and bisected by many rivers and streams.

The main town on the heights of the Escarpment is Lydenburg. It was founded over a century ago by a branch of the Great Trek, led by the doughty Hendrik Potgieter. His first settlement was further to the north, at Ohrigstad. By 1849, the village had been wiped out by fever and internal dissension, so the survivors trekked south to found Lydenburg, the 'Town of Suffering'.

Then, within a few years, came a new kind of settler. For it was in the Berg that the 'ash-blond' gold of Africa was first discovered in payable quantities. First at Spitskop, then at Geelhoutboom, sprawling communities of bearded miners sprang up. In August 1873, the President of the Transvaal Republic, François Burgers, paid a visit to the diggings at Geelhoutboom. He renamed the place Mac Mac, after the Scotsmen who predominated among the diggers. Then, in September of the same year, 'Wheelbarrow Alec' Patterson discovered a gold-laden stream in a nearby valley. Almost overnight, the village of Pilgrim's Rest was born. These were bonanza years for the miners, when fortunes were made and lost with breathtaking rapidity. Soon other fields were opened up, notably at Barberton further to the south, and in the great valley of 'De Kaap'. Later, after the surface levels had been cleaned out, a Rand mining company continued to work the deeper levels until a few years ago.

Now, after 100 years, the roar of the mines has gone. Pilgrim's Rest, with its picturesque, Victorian tin-roofed cottages, is a museum village. The pocketed and scarred valley below still bears witness to the energy of the miners. For visitors, it makes a starting point for an exploration of the more permanent wealth of the Berg – its scenic splendours. These range from the Mac Mac Falls, plunging 65 metres into the gorge, to the awesome Blyde River Canyon, with its 'Three Rondavels' formation. Here, too, is the Long Tom Pass. The highest motor road in the country, it was named after the Boer siege-gun which was hauled away over the mountain here, much to the ire of the pursuing British Army.

Below the cliffs of the Escarpment begins the Lowveld, reaching eastwards to the Lebombo mountains and the Mocambique border. Once this was a wilderness of sand, scrub and fever trees, of crocodile-infested rivers and malarial swamps. A deathtrap for hunters and explorers, it was ruefully abbreviated as MMBA – 'Miles and Miles of Bloody Africa!' Its ambiguous attractions were celebrated by Percy FitzPatrick in his classic, *Jock of the Bushveld*.

By the end of the last century, however, it seemed likely that the Lowveld might share the fate of so many of the country's wildlife areas, to be tamed and turned over to farmland. It was saved by the intervention of Paul Kruger, President of the Transvaal Republic. In 1898, he persuaded the Volksraad to set aside a tract of land as a sanctuary, the Sabie Game Reserve, later renamed the Kruger National Park. The second oldest park in Africa, it is 350 kilometres from north to south and covers nearly two million hectares. Besides the many thousands of the human species who pass through the park annually, there is a resident population including more than 7 000 elephants, 30 000 buffalo, and some twenty different species of antelope.

From old Africa, we fly westwards into the new. Crossing the Springbok Flats, we look down on the heart of the Highveld, in the cities of Pretoria and Johannesburg. The former is the country's administrative capital. It is set in a bowl of hills, once the headquarters of the renegade Mzilikazi. A fast-growing city, it is dominated by the Union Buildings and the Voortrekker Monument.

For sheer size, however, it is Johannesburg which holds the attention. It is an urban megapolis, spreading out from the artificial hills of the old mine-dumps and extending in a complex of other industrial towns across the low ridge of the Witwatersrand. Familiarly shortened to 'Joburg', to the mineworkers it is 'eGoldi'. For if much gold was mined in the heyday of the Drakensberg Escarpment, it was here on the Ridge of White Waters that the multi-billion rand jackpot was found. Barely 100 years ago there was little here beyond a few Boer farmhouses. The bleak, windswept ridge had long been tramped over by miners on their way to apparently better prospects. Then, in March 1886, two prospectors, Harrison and Walker, stumbled on gold reef on the surface.

Overnight, the Witwatersrand became the new El Dorado, as it continues to be. To date some 6 000-million tonnes of gold-bearing rock have been dug up here. By November 1886, the nucleus of the new gold rush town of Johannesburg had been surveyed and named. Soon an expansive and aggressive community of 'Uitlanders' had converged on the diggings. Led by the 'Gold Bugs', tycoons such as Cecil Rhodes, they were watched askance by the farmers of the Transvaal Republic under 'Oom Paul' Kruger. Tension between Boer and Briton built up through the last years of the century, culminating in the outbreak of the Boer War towards the close of 1899. The Transvaal Republic was joined by the Orange Free State in a bitter struggle for independence. Two years of war left a devastated land and 30 000 dead. El Dorado was acquired at a high price.

The sun and the wind rule the plain of the north-west Transvaal, once the stronghold of the Boer commandos. It is interrupted only by ranges such as the Magaliesberg and the Pilanesberg, scene of the Sun City resort. This region also includes the Marico District, the setting for Herman Charles Bosman's bucolic stories. The farms here grow a mixture of citrus, maize and tobacco. Across the border with the northern wing of the Cape is the town of Mafikeng. Once renowned for its siege during the Boer War, it has been given a new lease of life by the nearby capital of the Homeland of Bophuthatswana, Mmabatho.

Further south, across the Vaal River, lies the predominantly agricultural Orange Free State. It was founded during the Great Trek, with its capital at Bloemfontein. Rich alluvial land laid down by the Orange River supports a wide variety of crops, from wheat and maize, barley and lucerne, to potatoes, beans and onions. In the south, the region abuts the Karoo, and agriculture gives way to sheep farming.

If gold is the main thread in the history of the Transvaal, at Kimberley in the northern Cape it is diamonds. In 1869, diamonds were found embedded in the wall of a farmhouse at Bultfontein. Frenzied prospecting followed until, two years later, major new finds were made at Colesburg Koppie, a low rise in the middle of a near-desert. The Koppie was in fact the surface of a diamondiferous pipe. As with the gold, a raffish community of prospectors materialized as if from nowhere. At the height of the boom there were 30 000 miners at work. Their collective monument is the famous 'Big Hole', which at its final depth reached over a kilometre into the earth. Though surrounded by other workings and filled with water from a century of seepage, it continues to grip the imagination.

This is a harsh, sun-bleached landscape. As we turn west, the terrain becomes still bleaker. It is like a desert for most of the year in the Kalahari Gemsbok National Park, which occupies a vast wedge of land between South West Africa and Botswana. For the animals here, the herds of gemsbok, wildebeest and antelope, existence is a perpetual migration in search of water and grazing.

The main source of life in the northern Cape is the Orange River. Rising in the mountains of Lesotho, it traverses the entire subcontinent, winding westwards to the Atlantic. Along its banks, near Upington, is a large irrigation scheme, which incorporates vineyards. At the Augrabies Falls the river has carved out a 100m deep ravine from the rock. Both the falls and the surrounding area, with its characteristic 'kokerboom' trees, are part of the Augrabies Falls National Park.

Lessons in survival are seen, too, further south in Namaqualand. Here the local vegetation has learned to make the most of an ephemeral winter rainfall. From early August to the end of September, over 350 different species of wild flowers bloom, their transformation of the landscape as magical as it is brief.

If the shore is hot and dry for most of the year, the sea is cold. It is also rich in fish, supported by the 'upwelling' of nutrients in the Benguela Current. The West Coast fishing industry is centred on Saldanha Bay, in the Vredenburg Peninsula. The bay has had a long history since the days when it was used as a bolt-hole for pirates. At its entrance are islands, long the breeding grounds of jostling hordes of cormorants and gannets. The latter, unflatteringly called the 'mad goose' by the early Dutch, gave its name to Malgas Island. This was the scene of a furious guano rush in the 1830s. There was also whaling and sealing until legal protection of the animals was introduced. During the Second World War, Saldanha Bay was used by the British Navy after the German invasion of North Africa. The Allied warships limped in here for repairs during the Battle of the Atlantic. In recent years, other uses have been found for this versatile bay, with the construction of a large-scale iron ore export facility, handling some 20-million tonnes of ore a year.

It makes a sharp contrast with the nearby lagoon of Langebaan, enclosed by the Donkergat Peninsula, which runs southwards parallel to the shore for 15km. Surrounded by thick reed beds, this tranquil saltwater lagoon, recently declared a National Park, is one of the richest areas of bird and marine life on the coast. Another important wildlife preserve, offshore further south, is Dassen Island, home of the remaining population of jackass penguins.

The journey over South Africa comes full circle as we turn inland across the wheatlands of the Swartland to the mountains of the Western Cape seaboard. From the Cederberg and the Hex River mountains to the Hottentots Hollands, they seem to stand guard at the entrance to Africa. Three hundred years ago they saw the first inland settlements of the Dutch 'Free Burgher' farmers, first in Stellenbosch, then at Paarl, later still in the Boland itself, in the high valley of Tulbagh and in the Breede River and Olifants River regions. In all these places, the mountains made an idyllic setting for the local Cape Dutch architecture, the whitewashed gables and thatched roofs of the farmsteads shaded by oak trees. This image of tradition is completed by a further element, that of the wine. The original vines were imported and planted on a modest scale in the Table Bay area by the first Commander at the Cape, Jan van Riebeeck. Today the area boasts 14 official wine-making districts, each with its own character reflected in the wine.

From the air, we look down on the vineyards, changing colour as the season progresses, from fresh green in spring to deep russet at harvest time. It is a last image from a harvest of many horizons, from the Cape of Good Hope to the 'land of thirst', from the storm-beaten south coast to the last outpost of the elephants, in the Kruger Park. From them is distilled an essence, the magic and mystery which, from time immemorial have come 'out of Africa'.

The Photography

Coming up with the idea of photographing South Africa from the air is one thing; making all the arrangements and carrying out the assignment is quite another. Neil Sutherland, the photographer chosen, was already acknowledged as a top-class aerial photographer, with books on New York, America, Australia, Canada and Britain to his credit. He had gained considerable experience and recognition in both aerial and ground-level photography all over the world over some two decades. Even so, it took considerable planning to decide what to photograph of a country with which he was not familiar; when to photograph it in order to take advantage of the most perfect weather conditions, always necessary in aerial photography; what equipment to use, bearing in mind that he wanted to photograph not only the landscape, but also as much of the wildlife as possible; which aircraft to book, and for how long, as well as all the other smaller details of such a trip. He also needed to consult as many people, books and maps as he could find in order to be as prepared as possible.

The question of what equipment to use was quickly resolved. Neil had used various cameras for such projects in the past and had found that, while 35mm had a lot of advantages, being light, easy to manage, capable of taking motor drive and only needing reloading after every 36 frames, the quality that was required for large scale reproduction would be best achieved using the larger, roll film format. He therefore decided on the Pentax 6X7, a camera that can be used at eye level, like a 35mm camera, but which gives a much larger transparency. There is no such thing as the ideal camera, and the disadvantage of roll film cameras is, in addition to the extra weight and bulk involved, that they have to be reloaded more frequently than their smaller counterparts. In the case of the Pentax 6X7 this means after every ten exposures. So Neil decided to take two camera bodies and a variety of lenses, ranging from the 45mm wide-angle, for sweeping panoramas, to the 300mm telephoto, principally for wildlife photography. This last aspect of the trip gave some cause for concern, particularly about the equipment. Wild animals are very unlikely to stand still when being swooped on by a low-flying aircraft, and even if they do there is the problem of speed. However slowly a conventional aeroplane might be able to fly, it still travels at a considerable speed relative to the ground, and the lower it flies, the more its speed becomes apparent. With a hand-wound camera, Neil knew that he would only be able to take two, or at the most three, shots on each pass, and that by the time the aircraft could turn to make another run, the animal or animals would probably have disappeared.

The next problem, that of what to photograph and when, had to be settled in South Africa, and it could best be achieved in consultation with the pilot and people who knew the country well. The time of year, and the expected weather conditions, would play a large part in the success or otherwise of the trip. Weather for aerial photography really needs to be as perfect as possible. A beautiful day on the ground, warm and with hazy sunshine, may well prove quite unsuitable from the air. The haze will ruin the contrast so necessary for this type of photography and make everything appear flat and lifeless. Even puffy white clouds that so ideally complement a blue sky will cast huge shadows on the ground over which the photographer is working. After talking to various people in South Africa it was finally decided that October and November would be the most likely months for the required conditions.

If the choice of equipment was relatively easy, the choice of pilot was not. Aerial photography demands particular flying skills and, most important, an understanding of the aims of the photographer. The pilot needs to be able to handle the aircraft in an unusual way, often flying at 90 degrees to the normal attitude to make photography possible. He needs to be well acquainted with the countryside he will be covering, where the fuelling stops are located, and so on, and he must be able to land the aeroplane on, and take off from, such unusual airstrips as a local golf course!

That Neil accomplished the photography successfully is proven in the pictures on the following pages. A truly superb collection of photographs, they surely speak for themselves. That he owes a great deal to the expertise and cooperation of Jan Viljoen, the pilot, Neil readily and gratefully acknowledges, and it is the pilot's recollections of the assignment which now continue the story.

The South African Tourism Board contacted the offices of TROPAIR to arrange a meeting between them and Hanni Edmonds, of Colour Library Books, to discuss the possibility of a photographer being taken up at a later stage to photograph South Africa from the air. The meeting was set for the 3rd September 1985, with TROPAIR completely in the dark as to the extent of the exercise. Their representatives met Mrs Edmonds and Geraldine Murray of SATOUR at a luncheon at Wonderboom aerodrome. Mrs Edmonds outlined her company's plans and TROPAIR started to realise that this was no ordinary tourist photographer wanting a flip. The publishers, it turned out, wanted to produce a book on the whole of South Africa as seen from the air!

TROPAIR anticipated encountering problems in obtaining permission to overfly certain areas in the country, and meetings with government departments were, therefore, arranged. After discussions with senior officials of the departments of Defence, Transport, Civil Aviation, Parks Board and other parties concerned, outlining the objectives of the book, permission was given and TROPAIR began organizing the tour in detail. It is gratifying to add that the concept was well received by all the relevant departments and the venture was given their full support at all times.

Talks with Geoff Cooper of Central News Agency highlighted the areas that were expected to be covered and also what exactly was demanded from TROPAIR. Collecting numerous books, pamphlets, brochures and maps, and poring over the information, the team tried to reconcile places of beauty and splendour on the ground with possible similar and better shots from the air. It took some time to compile all the data that were considered to be important into a feasible itinerary. The tour would take a route from Cape Town covering almost all of the eastern coastline of South Africa, zig-zagging from one town to another. The route thus planned, the next step was for the pilot and the photographer to put their heads together to work out the practicalities of the task ahead – the actual photographing from the aeroplane. Jan Viljoen went to England to meet the photographer to discuss all the technicalities.

It was decided that the ideal aeroplane would be a Cessna 177 Cardinal with fixed undercarriage. It has a 180 horsepower motor fitted with a variable pitch propeller and seats 4 people. It is capable of flying at speeds between 112kph (70mph) and 217kph (135mph). The planners recognized that, in many ways, a helicopter would be more suitable but, because of the distances to be covered and the fact that using a helicopter would be some three to four times more expensive, it was ruled out.

The endurance of the Cessna is a good six hours and it can cover, at normal cruising speed, about 1 450km (900 miles) on a full tank. The Cardinal is a highwing aircraft with no wing struts, and with the two front seats being slightly in front of the wing it was a most suitable aircraft for the job.

A big, square section of the front starboard window was removed and fitted with hinges so that it could easily be taken out and replaced as and when required, thus enabling Neil to manoeuvre unhindered. This arrangement proved very suitable, apart from losing the first window somewhere near Cape Point when the slipstream got hold of it.

There were times when Jan felt that the 180 horses providing the thrust were not enough – especially during low level, very windy conditions where at least 400 horses would have been comforting but, in general, this aircraft, which is also used by South Africa's National Road Safety Council, proved to be fully up to the requirements of the job.

To make up for the very high wind noise when flying with the window removed, Jan used earphones throughout and Neil was equipped with earplugs. They also made good use of the shoulder straps provided.

South Africa is a big country and covering the entire area inevitably meant that the team would be running into bad weather of some sort, particularly thunderstorms – storms are prevalent in October – fog, mist, strong winds or ordinary overcast skies. They hoped for 75 per cent good weather because Neil would require full sunlight for almost all of his pictures. As it turned out, they eventually enjoyed 85 per cent good weather.

The planned route was expected to take 34 days – weather permitting – and would be from Cape Town in the south up the east coastline, zig-zagging inland, to the most northerly border in the Kruger National Park; to central South Africa; to the extreme west as far as the Kalahari Desert and down the western coastline to finish back at Cape Town.

They covered roughly 23 000 kilometers (14,300 miles) in 123 hours of flying which took them over terrains of extreme opposites – from the high mountains of the Drakensberg, the plains of the Karoo, the green of Natal, the stark beauty of the emptiness of the Kalahari Desert, the never ending agricultural lands in the Orange Free State, to the tranquillity of the game parks and the breathtaking beauty of the Cape.

Because of the high wind noise from the open window in the aircraft, conversation was not possible, and Neil and Jan had to resort to sign language most of the time. After only a couple of days both pilot and photographer got to know, more or less, the other's requirements and limitations, which cut out a lot of unnecessary communication (there was no communication from Neil's side when the weather was bad as he closed both his camera and his mouth!). At night, when the debriefing of the day's work was done, Jan had to translate all the weather forecasts for the next day. Their hopes for good weather overruled most other considerations.

Flying over South Africa almost non-stop for 34 days and expecting not to encounter bad weather and difficult flying conditions is asking too much. Starting at Cape Town, they experienced the usual strong south easterly winds, which caused a small amount of turbulence in the mountain area, but nothing that had not been anticipated or could not be handled. En route from Aliwal North to the Wild Coast, it was necessary to fly by instruments for 90 minutes, which, ideally, one would prefer not to do in a single-engined aircraft. Probably the most difficult flying was experienced on the south coast of Natal with a gale force wind of 40 knots blowing, making it necessary to fly at 152m (500ft) or lower. This was the time that the 180 horses of the aircraft were not enough, and on a day like this it was impossible for them to penetrate the Drakensberg. Apart from Neil not being able to stabilise his equipment, the aircraft was almost uncontrollable. At Cape Agulhas the most extraordinary winds made it almost impossible to fly in the way necessary for Neil to take pictures. There was a cloud base of 30m (100ft) and very strong winds, possibly created by the joining of the warm and the cold currents, causing windsheer, a phenomenon in which winds of different speeds meet, and which is an experience better to miss!

From the one extreme they went to the other, where winds were of no concern. On one occasion, the runway was washed away and they had to make do with what was left, testing the performance and capability of the little aircraft, and the pilot, to the extreme. There was also the occasion of landing urgently on the fairway of a golf course to use their toilet facilities, and where the subsequent take-off was accomplished, though barely missing golfers on the eighth green! In the Western Cape they encountered a heatwave where temperatures up to 49deg C were tabled, and in the Kalahari temperatures on the gauges ran into the red – of both aircraft and passengers! Then there was the occasion in the desert when Neil and Jan had to carry three 25-litre fuel cans 250m (273yds) in the middle of a game park! At the end the photographer, pilot and aircraft came out with no scars – a feat worthy of mention, especially after low passings over a nudist park while trying to picture the splendour of the Cape coast!

They stayed in 17 hotels during the 34 days, experiencing everything from 'bokkons' (dried fish) at Paternoster, to the best cuisine in the best hotels, for which they warmly salute Southern Sun and SATOUR.

Landing was accomplished on 30 different landing strips – some of them barely noticeable – from the longest runway in the southern hemisphere, at Upington, and the riverbed at Twee Riviere, to the golf course par five at Sabie River Bungalows and the golf course at Tzaneen (one of the most beautiful 18th holes in the world), sans South Africa's famous Gary Player. And there was the team's gratitude for the wonderful co-operation they received from all the air traffic controllers throughout the entire trip.

Overall, both Jan and Neil agree that this was a unique experience and one to be savoured – an opportunity to cover most of a beautiful country, and for each to work with a very professional counterpart. Both of them feel that they have learned a great deal from the challenge and have emerged from it enriched by the experience.

Table Mountain, Cape Town and Table Bay.

Facing page: the broad Heerengracht and the curve of Western Boulevard leading into Table Bay Boulevard, on the Foreshore in Cape Town Central Area. The Foreshore, reclaimed through the dredging of Table Bay in order to build Duncan Dock, was once a rocky bay whose shoreline is marked by the three ornamental ponds on the Heerengracht.
Above: Green Point, and part of the Sea Point area of Cape Town. Overleaf: (left) sunset behind Table Mountain and Lion's Head. The Rhodes Memorial (right) stands on the slopes of Devil's Peak in Groote Schuur estate, Cape Town.

Above: the sugar-loaf peak of Lion's Head rises 669 metres above the Sea Point area of Cape Town.
Facing page: tower blocks in central Cape Town dwarf the Grand Parade and the old, sandstone city hall, completed in 1905. Beyond lies the green of the Company's Garden and De Waal Park. Overleaf: (left) the rocky Atlantic shore of Clifton Bay, backed by the peaks of the Twelve Apostles. Right: the seawater pool on Sea Point Promenade, backed by luxury hotels and apartments lining Beach Road.

Above: Sea Point. Facing page: a sports arena near Green Point. Overleaf: (left) Camps Bay and the Twelve Apostles and (right) rugged rocks on the shoreline at Sea Point.

Previous pages: Sea Point (left) is the liveliest and most densely populated of Cape Town's suburbs. Right: one of the four sheltered beaches of Clifton Bay. Above: nestling amongst granite boulders at the foot of a peak called Little Lion's Head is Llandudno, where the rusting wreck of a ship testifies to the treacherous combination of strong winds and jagged rocks. Camps Bay (facing page) is also exposed to the strong south-east wind, yet it is usually sunny and popular with bathers and picnickers.

Previous pages: Lion's Head (left) is seen towering majestically over the metropolis and (right) is a spectacular view of the Cape Peninsula, which stretches south for 75 kilometres. In the past, from the summit of Lion's Head (above), a watchman would signal approaching ships by firing a cannon. Today, the mountain is mainly appreciated for its beauty alone. Facing page: from Table Mountain, one has a breathtaking view of the city with the harbour beyond. Overleaf: (left) Sea Point and (right) a view south, towards the Hout Bay area.

Previous pages, left: Cape Town University in the foreground, with Devil's Peak and the harbour beyond. Previous pages, right: a lakeside near Muizenburg, which has been a fashionable place to live since the turn of the century. The lovely sandy shore of Chapman's Bay, in the foreground (above), was named after a seaman, John Chapman, and is the earliest surviving English place name. With its mountainous setting and pleasing curve, Hout Bay (facing page) has great beauty as well as a bustling atmosphere created by its fishing industry.

One of the most breathtaking scenic drives in South Africa is Chapman's Peak Drive (previous pages), which, carving its way through the rich colours of Table Mountain, commands marvellous views of Hout Bay and Chapman's Bay. These pages: the colours of the sea turn to frothy white at the shoreline of Cape Point, on which a lighthouse seems precariously perched. Overleaf: (left) with its white, sandy beaches and safe waters warmed by the currents of False Bay, Muizenburg is a favourite seaside recreational area. Kalk Bay (right) with its picturesque fishing harbour.

Above: Chapman's Bay and Chapman's Peak. Facing page: the University of Cape Town, which occupies some of the fine buildings on the Groote Schuur estate of Cecil Rhodes, enjoys a splendid location on the slopes of Devil's Peak.
Overleaf: (left) the village of Hermanus is well known as a fishing resort and its old fishing harbour, shown in the foreground, has been restored and turned into a national monument. Right: the town of Paarl, the 'pearl' of the Berg River Valley, in the Western Cape.

With its rich soil, warm climate and easy access to a harbour, the Berg River Valley was a natural starting point for South Africa's fruit export industry. Near Paarl (above) wine is made from local grapes, which, along with apples, are the major fruit grown in the area. Facing page: the Boschendal estate, one of the handsome Rhodes Fruit Farms, was bought by Cecil Rhodes in 1896, and has a fine vineyard as well as farm buildings exhibiting Cape-Dutch architecture. The town of Franschhoek (overleaf) provides a market for the surrounding farms.

Stellenbosch, with its beautifully preserved buildings, is known as 'the town of oaks' and is South Africa's oldest town.
Facing page: the Lanzerac winery. Overleaf: (left) the University of Stellenbosch. Overleaf right: one of the most
famous and luxurious express trains in the world is the Blue Train, which started running in the 1920s and still travels
the main line from Cape Town to Johannesburg and Pretoria and back.

The Breë River Valley is the largest of the wine and fruit producing regions in the Western Cape. Worcester (above), the valley's main town, is a bustling commercial and industrial centre. In autumn, the Hex River Valley (facing page) is ablaze with colour as the leaves on the grapevines turn a deep red. The valley is densely covered with over 6,000,000 vines producing the large, strong, black barlinka grapes which constitute most of South Africa's grape export. Overleaf left: the Blue Train speeds through the Hex River Valley. Overleaf right: countryside near Wellington.

When early settlers came across the valley in which Wellington (these pages) now lies, they believed they had reached the farthest limit of civilization. The town has grown considerably since its foundation, and in 1873 became an important educational centre with the establishment of the Huguenot College. Overleaf: (right) the lovely countryside surrounding Caledon (left), which is known for its chalybeate baths and its beautiful wild flower reserve.

Apart from its flourishing wool and grain farms and wild-flower cultivation, Bredasdorp (facing page) is known for its interesting local history museum. Northwest of Bredasdorp is the little town of Napier (above), which was named after Governor Sir George Napier.

The heartland of South Africa is a 250,000-square-kilometre stretch of hot, dry land called the Great Karoo. One of the important characteristics of the region is its invigorating and health-giving air, which led to the development of Matjiesfontein (above). This once fashionable Victorian health and holiday resort had to cater for a different kind of customer after the outbreak of the Boer War, when it became a British Remount Camp. Facing page: the Witteberge mountain range.

Previous pages: situated at the western end of the Swartberg Mountains are the towns of Ladismith (left) and Calitzdorp (right), which are both known for ostrich farming, the former having shared in the ostrich feather boom of the late 1800s. The centre of this boom was at Oudtshoorn (above), which is situated on the fertile land of the Little Karoo, and still has ostrich farms, such as that shown (facing page), which are still the world's most successful breeders of these curious birds.

Below, bottom left and facing page: the romantic coastline of Wilderness, and (right and bottom right) Mossel Bay, which is the start of the Garden Route, a stretch of luxuriant coastline enhanced by a glorious variety of trees and flowers. Overleaf: (left) George, the principal town of the Garden Route, and (right) Plettenberg Bay, featuring the Beacon Island Hotel.

Previous pages: (left) the Heads, two sandstone cliffs which guard the narrow inlet leading to Knysna Lagoon, and (right) the golden, sandy beach on Walker Point. Beacon Island (above) derives its name from the beacon that Governor Plettenberg placed on the land that he claimed as the possession of the Dutch East India Company. Since then the island has been the site of a Norwegian whaling station and is now a popular holiday resort, sporting a modern hotel which offers an exciting location on the jagged, seaworn rocks. Facing page: a rugged part of the coastline near Knysna.

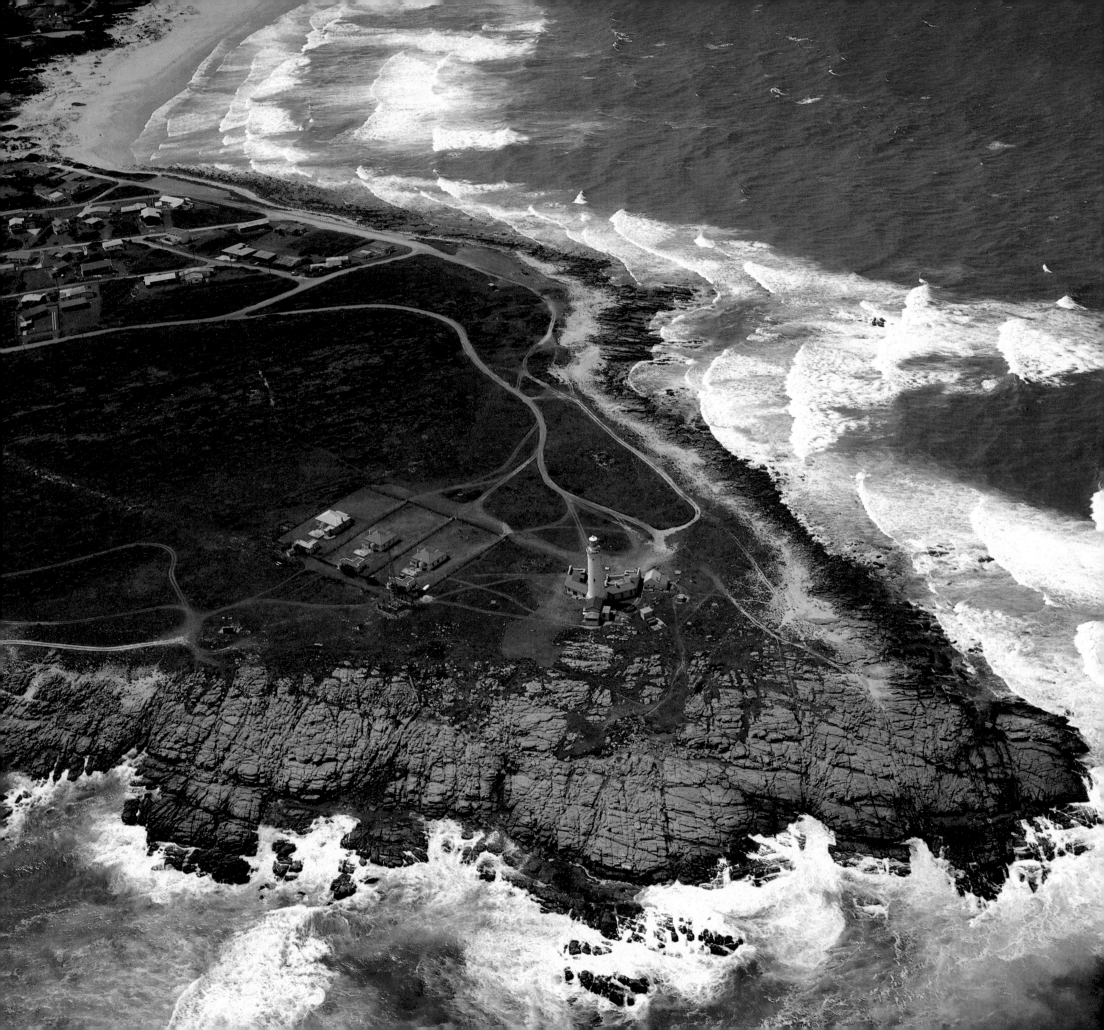

Previous pages: (left) a lighthouse affords dramatic views of the raging waves assailing Cape St. Francis. Right: the Paul Sauer Bridge, which spans the spectacular gorge of the Storms River. Above: the land fragments into a chain of jewels scattered along the coastline of the Tsitsikama Forest and Coastal National Parks. Facing page: luxury homes at Sea Vista enjoy views of St Francis Bay.

Previous pages: aerial views of the busy harbour and downtown area of Port Elizabeth, the Cape's second city and South Africa's third largest port. The town was named after the wife of Sir Rufane Donkin, who was acting governor of the Cape in the early 1800s. Above: Avontuur, in the luxuriant, fruit producing valley of the Langkloof. The Olifants River (facing page) emerges from the mysterious-looking Grootswartberge, or 'great black mountains'. Overleaf: (left) Beaufort West, the largest town in the Karoo, and (right) the pretty town of Graaff-Reinet, known as the 'gem of the Karoo'.

Transkei has a rugged, magical shoreline called the Wild Coast (these pages), which is a 250-kilometre stretch of unspoilt beaches, green, grass-covered cliffs and bays of turbulent, blue water. Below: the Wild Coast Sun Hotel and (bottom left) the Umtamvuna River, near Transkei's northern border.

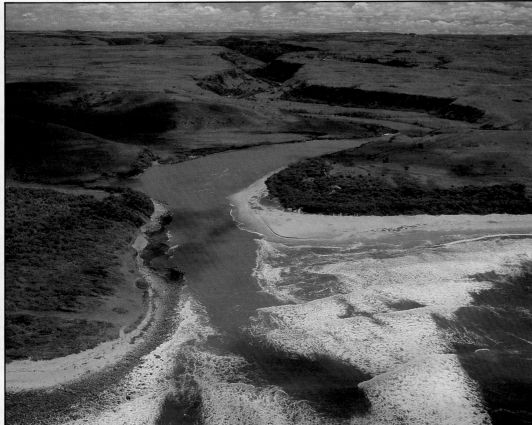

The Umtamvuna River (previous pages) twists and turns through lush countryside on its route from the Ingeli Mountains to the sea. South of Durban, the coast of Natal is blessed with high rainfall, rich soil and temperatures ranging from warm to hot and humid. Consequently, the vegetation is luxuriant and the area has become one of South Africa's favourite holiday playgrounds, offering superbly situated resorts such as San Lameer (facing page), near Margate, and the luxury homes (above) on the rugged coast near Palm Beach.

Port Shepstone (left), situated at the mouth of the great Umzimkulu River, is a major town on the south coast of Natal. Holiday-makers flock to the charming town of Scottburgh (remaining pictures), where they can bathe safely in the warm waters of Scott's Bay. Facing page: an impressive array of modern hotels indicates the popularity of the lovely resort of Umhlanga Rocks.

Left and below: Umhlanga Rocks. Remaining pictures and facing page: with its ideal location on the shores of Port Natal, Durban is the main port of South Africa, handling a large proportion of its cargo. As it is also one of the world's most beautiful maritime cities, it has become a very successful holiday resort and is the perfect place to mix business with pleasure.

Previous page, left: the Durban campus of the University of Natal, which, from its hilltop location, commands spectacular views of the city. Previous page, right: the Durban seafront is a fun-lover's paradise, with golden sand, amusement facilities, a relaxed atmosphere and the warm waters of the Indian Ocean. The attractive homes in Durban's suburbs (these pages) are sheltered by tree-lined avenues and shady gardens which balance and contrast the city's high-rise downtown area.

Previous pages: (left) Umhlanga Rocks and (right) the coastline north of Durban, where the hubbub of the city gives way to the romantic, desolate beauty of secluded bays and green, unspoilt hills. A similarly verdant landscape is found along the coast, further north, in the area of Mtunzini (these pages), where the dunes are densely forested and dotted with lakelets. Although very beautiful, this area has only one holiday resort, as the beaches are steeply shelved and the sea is largely unprotected from sharks.

Previous page, left: along the coast from Durban to the Tugela River, the land is covered with the vibrant green of sugar cane plantations. This crop was brought from Mauritius in the mid-1800s and has grown into an industry producing over two million tons of sugar a year. One of South Africa's most breathtaking sights is the Valley of a Thousand Hills (right, below and previous page right), which is aptly named, for around the main valley of the Umgeni River myriad undulating hills and vales stretch to the horizon. The lush slopes, adorned with lilies and acacias, are dotted with the white-roofed dwellings of the Debe tribe. The Howick Falls (bottom right) are a major tourist attraction along the Umgeni River. Pietermaritzburg (facing page) is the provincial capital of Natal and was built in the mid-1800s by the Voortrekkers, who named it after their two leaders Piet Retief and Gert Maritz. It is a charming city with wide streets, luxuriant gardens and fine buildings, many of which are constructed from the characteristic, bright red brick.

Previous pages: (left) burning stubble, northwest of Durban and (right) Greytown, which is often blanketed by cloud and mist brought by the moist winds from the Indian Ocean. The Zulu name for the Tugela River, Natal's principal river, is 'Thukela' which means 'something that startles' and, as it carves a tortuous route through its magnificent valley, it is indeed an awesome spectacle. On the river's long journey to the Indian Ocean it irrigates a number of towns, such as Tugela Ferry (facing page). Above: beef cattle in Helpmekaar.

Previous pages, left: the coal mining town of Dundee, and (previous page, right) Newcastle, which was established as a trade and administrative centre for north Natal in 1864. Left: farmland west of Newcastle. Remaining pictures: attractive countryside surrounding the town of Harrismith (facing page), centre of the eastern Orange Free State.

During the Anglo-Boer War an event took place that immortalised the town of Ladysmith (right and bottom right). Although heavily outnumbered, the Boers succeeded in driving the British into the town and holding them under siege for 120 days. The monuments and cemeteries, along with many museum relics, recall the siege and the brave and skilful strategy of the Boers. Below: the Tugela River Valley. Van Reenens Pass (facing page) crosses the Drakensberg range at the border of northern Natal and the Orange Free State. A pass was planned in the 1850s, when trade was booming, and a link between the provinces became vital. However, it seemed improbable that a suitable route would be found until a farmer, Frans Van Reenen, showed road engineers the path over the mountains which he took when driving his livestock to market. Today, the pass continues to be of great convenience to the traveller, and is also appreciated as a route of great scenic beauty, commanding fine views from its summit, Windy Corner, 1,680 metres above sea level.

Below: Zulu farmhouses. Right and bottom left: Sugar trains transporting cane from the fields to processing plants. Facing page: the spirit of tribal life is recreated in the Zululand Safari Lodge Hotel, which includes an example of a typical kraal (bottom right), with its carefully thatched, round huts.

11 - 18 JULY 87

The coast of Tongaland is not only rich in beauty but also in wildlife: the sea offers an abundance of fish and some rare turtles, and the shore boasts a variety of interesting birds. Much of the coast is protected as national parkland, such as the lovely Kosi Bay area (right and facing page) and (remaining pictures) Sodwana Bay National Park.

Previous pages: St Lucia Estuary. The harbour at Richards Bay (above) was built to relieve Durban of the increase in cargo that resulted from South Africa's expansion after World War II. The harbour's opening in 1976 encouraged the development of many industrial plants (remaining pictures). Facing page: Zululand University in Empangeni.

Many species of wild animal have long been attracted to the grassland which, since the turn of the century, has been the Hluhluwe Game Reserve (this page). Today, visitors enjoy viewing an astounding variety of creatures, such as rhino, giraffe, lion and crocodile, in their natural habitat. Nature lovers also marvel at the landscape itself, which comprises rolling hills and valleys covered in lush grass and dense forests, through which runs the lovely Hluhluwe River. Facing page: pens at a cattle auction at Bigala, near the Mkuzi Game Reserve, which contains a fine selection of wildlife, as well as some interesting plant life. Overleaf left: land clearance near Piet Retief, which was almost totally destroyed during the Boer War but is now a busy town with a flourishing timber and paper-making industry. Sugar cane fields at Pongola (overleaf right) are irrigated by the Pongola River, which is Tongaland's principal waterway.

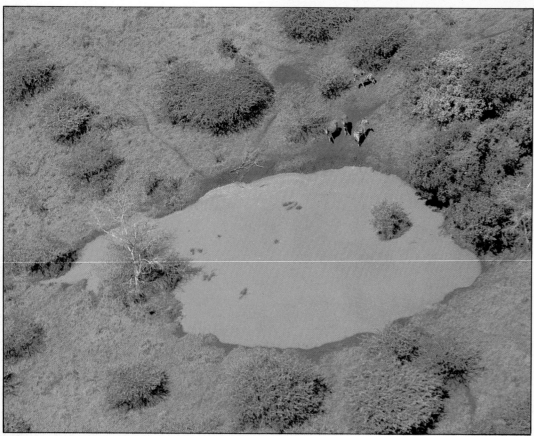

For a brief period during the late 1800s, the town of Amsterdam (above) was the scene of an attempt by the Scot, Alexander McCorkindale, to recreate a piece of Scotland in the eastern Transvaal. He planned to import 300 Scots to build new farms and towns and to establish Amsterdam, or Roburnia as he named it, as the capital of this settlement. Although his efforts failed on the whole, due to lack of funds, the first 50 Scots to arrive left a legacy by working hard and establishing some fine farms. Facing page: Piet Retief.

Above: a saw-mill at Piet Retief. Facing page: tree plantations at Warburton. In the late 1800s, Graham Barber and two of his cousins found a glittering reef of gold in the broad, verdant De Kaap Valley. The boom town of Barberton was born (overleaf left) and rapidly became a den of iniquity, with racketeers indulging in gambling, heavy drinking and gunplay. Today, it is a charming town, with flowering trees lining streets of fine, old buildings, yet it still has the lingering atmosphere of its lively past. Overleaf right: Nelspruit, one of South Africa's largest producers of citrus fruits.

Previous pages: when gold was found in the De Kaap Valley, the nearby town of Badplaas (left) became well known for its medicinal hot sulphur spring and it is now a popular resort. Right: the town of White River, which was originally a settlement for demobilized soldiers after the Boer War. Above: banana plantations at Hazyview, just north of White River. Facing page: mauve jacaranda trees decorate the gardens of the luxury Pine Lake Inn, at White River. Overleaf: (left) the pretty town of Sabie and (right) a valley between Sabie and Lydenburg.

Previous pages, left: the town of Lydenburg, which means 'town of suffering' and was named thus due to the traumas of its first settlers, who founded the town after leaving their nearby hometown of Ohrigstad, which was de-populated by malaria. Previous pages, right: Pilgrim's Rest was a gold mining town that boomed in the late 1800s and is now a living museum, with several active prospectors and a strong atmosphere of the gold-rush days. These pages: the fertile valley of Ohrigstad, which was resettled in the 1920s after its malaria-induced 'death' in the late 1800s.

The Blyde River Canyon (previous pages), on the eastern escarpment of the Drakensberg, ranks as one of South Africa's most beautiful natural wonders. The river lies roughly 800 metres below the summit of the cliffs and winds its way through the magnificent green gorge which is rich in rare plant life and is the home of many wild animals, such as leopards, lynxes and baboons. Above: Route 71 cuts through vast stretches of forest between Tzaneen and Phalaborwa. The famous Kruger National Park (facing page), Africa's first wildlife reserve, was established in 1898 by President Paul Kruger. It has the greatest variety of animals in any African game park and, with its fine scenery and plant life, continues to be a major attraction.

For nearly a century, gold has been South Africa's major source of wealth, and mines (right and facing page) stretch for roughly 500 kilometres across the land, in what has become known as the 'Golden Arc'. Other minerals, such as copper and phosphate (bottom left), are found beneath the country's fertile soil. Bottom right: a productive citrus farm.

Top right: an emerald mine near Gravelotte. Above and left: the Letsitele citrus estate, which is ablaze with colour in autumn, when the orange trees are laden with ripe fruit and scented blossom. Top left and facing page: workers on a tomato plantation. Overleaf: (left) tobacco fields and (right) a tomato farm.

The town of Tzaneen (top pictures) was established as a centre for the agricultural land of the Letaba River valley. Tea (previous pages) is one of the major crops grown in this fertile region, in which irrigation is assisted by the Ebenezer Dam (above and facing page). Left: a saw mill at Vergelegen.

Previous pages: (left) the Zion City Moria, seat of the Zion Christian Church, which has the largest Black following in South Africa and (right) Turfloop University of the North, which is of interest architecturally as it combines a modern structure with traditional African design. Above: the Coach House near Tzaneen. Facing page: the magnificent Letaba citrus estate, one of the largest citrus farms in the world. Overleaf: a copper mine at the town of Messina (left), which has long been the centre for South Africa's copper industry, and lies next to the Zimbabwe border (right).

Mighty, yet lovable, the African elephant strolls in herds (facing page) and small groups (overleaf pages) through the stunning landscape (above) of Kruger National Park. These massive creatures prefer to inhabit the northern end of the park and number over 7,500 in total. Over 3 per cent of South Africa's land mass is occupied by game reserves and the South Africa Nature Foundation continues to finance new conservation projects, such as the re-introduction of a species to areas where it has become extinct, thus undoing the damage done by hunters in the 19th century.

In the early 18th century a tribe from what is now Zimbabwe settled in the fertile land of a mountain range they called Venda, meaning 'the pleasant place'. One of the attractions of Vendaland (above and facing page) is the Fundudzi Lake (top left) which is allegedly the home of a giant python god of fertility. Remaining pictures: Pietersburg, showing (left) a silicon mine.

Previous pages: agriculture enhances the beauty of the northern Transvaal, which, at the vast citrus farm in Zebediela (left), is transformed into a patchwork of green and gold. The town of Potgietersrus (these pages) was named after the Voortrekker Commandant-General Piet Potgieter, who was killed while holding 2,000 Tlou tribesmen under siege in the Makapansgat Caves. This neat, modern town has an interesting cultural history museum and is well known for its glorious sub-tropical gardens. Overleaf: (left) sand is removed from the land near Ellisras (right), a small town approximately 28 kilometres from the Botswana border.

Much modern technology is employed in the land around Ellisras, which is the site of the Escom Power Plant (top left) and open cast coal mining (above and top right). Right: an asbestos mine near Northam. Facing page: the iron ore mine at Thabazimbi. Overleaf pages: the luxury Sun City resort in Bophuthatswana.

Previous and overleaf pages: farming activity in the golden land of the western Transvaal. Above: the sports stadium at Mmabatho, which was created as the capital of Bophuthatswana just before the republic gained independence. Facing page: just south of Mmabatho is the famous town of Mafikeng (formerly known as Mafeking), which was held under siege by Colonel R.S.S. Baden-Powell and his men. The siege, noted for its amiability and comparitive non-violence, lasted for roughly seven months and, during this time, Baden-Powell decided to use the young boys of Mafikeng to execute various non-combatant tasks. This kept them out of trouble, and they proved to be strong and able; the idea of the Boy Scout movement was born to Baden-Powell during this time.

Top right: Mmabatho sports stadium. The modern design of the Bophuthatswana Government Offices in Mmabatho (top left and facing page) decorates the stark, parched landscape. Similar design motifs enhance the home (above) of Bophuthatswana's President and Mafikeng's luxury Mmabatho Sun hotel (left).

A herd of cattle (above) is dwarfed by the vastness of the western Transvaal's agricultural land (facing page and overleaf pages). South Africa has a range of climates, varying from semi-desert to sub-tropical, therefore almost any kind of crop can be grown and livestock reared for a number of uses. However, as most of the country tends to be dry, irrigation is often necessary.

The town of Rustenburg (above) lies in a pleasant, tree-filled valley overlooked by the Magaliesberg range. Holiday-makers are attracted by its agreeable climate and the nearby Boekenhoutfontein Farm, which was the home of Paul Kruger. Facing page: Lichtenburg, which in the 1920s was stormed by literally thousands of fortune hunters following the discovery of diamonds in the area. Pretoria (overleaf) is the administrative capital of South Africa and the seat of the Provincial Administration of the Transvaal. Apart from its national importance, it is a city of rare beauty, with a profusion of jacaranda trees and some fine old buildings such as the neoclassical Union Buildings (right), which are surrounded by magnificent landscaped gardens.

KRONENDAL

MAGGA

Previous pages, left: Pretoria, featuring the massive Voortrekker Monument, which was designed by Gerhard Moerdyk and commemorates the Great Trek, during which about 6,000 Afrikaner farmers left the Cape Colony and headed north to establish themselves in the Orange Free State, Natal and the Transvaal. The impressive granite monument contains many beautiful works of art depicting the Trek and its heroes, including the great statues of Piet Retief and Andries Pretorius, which guard two corners of the monument. Previous page right: the University of South Africa, with the glittering, modern towers of the downtown area beyond. Facing page: the Union Buildings in their verdant surroundings. Above: the Loftus Versfeld Sports Stadium. Overleaf pages: aerial views of Pretoria.

KRONENDAL

HOSSEY
BLDG

Aerial views of Pretoria, featuring (previous page left) the awesome face of the Iscor steelworks, which assumes a more romantic aspect in the soft half-light. Previous page right: the University of Pretoria, which is the Republic's largest full-time university and also an important cultural centre, housing the Aula theatre complex. These pages: near the Union Buildings are found a number of attractive ministerial houses. Their ornate gardens are enhanced by a sprinkling of the mauve jacaranda blossom that characterises Pretoria and has led to the epithet 'the jacaranda city'. Overleaf: Iscor (left) is one of South Africa's largest industrial concerns. Overleaf right: the Black town of Atteridgeville west of Pretoria.

RIETONDALE PARK

KN6

LIBERTAS

GEORGE WASHINGTON

WENLOCK

COLROYN

Above: the beautiful Hartbeespoort Dam area, west of Pretoria. Facing page: the Royal Johannesburg Golf Club enjoys some green space, away from the built-up bustle of Johannesburg. This great, modern metropolis began life as a gold-mining boom town and, having continued to boom, has become the Republic's richest city and the centre of its finance and commerce. Today, when looking at Johannesburg (overleaf pages) one can imagine the variety of commercial and industrial activity that creates its wealth. However, there are constant reminders of the foundations of this prosperity in the huge yellow and white mountains of tailings (right) from the gold mines on the productive reef of the Witwatersrand.

The face of downtown Johannesburg (these pages) is always changing, as new and exciting modern structures seem to spring up almost overnight. Circular towers, such as the one shown (above), contrast the angular blocks that rise from the city's neat grid system. In the spring, jacaranda trees bring splashes of colour to the network of long, straight streets and the whole scene is overlooked by the J.G. Strijdom Post Office Tower (facing page right of centre, and overleaf right), which reaches a giant 269 metres into the sky. Overleaf left: The Wanderers' Golf Club with next to it (middle distance) The Wanderers' Club with its playing fields and famous cricket stadium.

In the heart of Johannesburg (these pages) is the massive Ellis Park Stadium (facing page), which can seat over 70,000 spectators and is the home of the Transvaal Rugby Union. Overleaf: (left) a Johannesburg suburb and (right) a gold mine near Krugersdorp, which was originally the Paardekraal farm where, in December 1880, over 6,000 men gathered together and swore to fight for the independence of the Transvaal, erecting a monument to pledge their faith. One of their leaders was Paul Kruger and, following the successful First War of Independence, he was appointed President of the restored republic. A few years later, following the discovery of gold on the Paardekraal farm, the town of Krugersdorp was created and named after the President.

Soweto (previous pages) is one of South Africa's largest urban complexes, housing over a million people from a variety of ethnic groups. Top left: Premier Mine, where the Cullinan Diamond, at that time the world's largest, was found in 1905. Top right: feed lots near Middleburg. Right: open cast coal mining near Witbank. Above: the Kriel Power Station, near Bethal. Facing page: the little village of Charl Cilliers, east of Bethal.

Previous pages: (left) the industrial area at Witbank and (right) Vereeniging, where the power of the Vaal River, together with local coal, is employed at five great thermal power stations, producing electricity for the entire Witwatersrand. The town's considerable industrial expansion began with the production of steel by USCO, the Union Steel Corporation, which has joined ISCOR, and occupies the huge site (above). Facing page: man-made mountains of tailings tower over the gold mining town of Stilfontein.

For many years the prairies of South Africa's central plateau, the Orange Free State (these pages), have yielded their treasures to man. Hunters found the land swarming with vast herds of game, farmers of the Great Trek found the soil could nourish a variety of crops and, in the 1940s, rich deposits of coal, gold and diamonds were found there. Facing page: a farmstead enjoys the beauty and fertility of the land near Kroonstad. Above: agriculture near Odendaalsrus, which was transformed from a quiet, isolated village into a famous, frenzied boom town when large gold deposits were discovered nearby. Overleaf: (left) a gold mining area at Welkom and (right) a flock of flamingoes, giving a fine example of the sheer abundance of the Orange Free State's wildlife.

The lovely town of Clarens (facing page) was named in honour of Paul Kruger, who died in Clarens in Switzerland in 1904. Nearby is the Golden Gate Highland National Park (above), where the picturesque landscape is distinguished by beautifully coloured sandstone formations. These have been eroded over the years, creating extraordinary shapes such as 'Gladstone's Nose', a giant cliff that has been transformed by the elements into the contours of a human face. Overleaf pages: the spectacular Drakensberg Range.

The Royal Natal National Park (these pages), lies at the northern end of Natal's Drakensberg Range, at the foot of the beautiful Mont-aux-Sources, where many rivers have their source. One such river, the Tugela, provides some of the park's spectacular scenery, such as the series of waterfalls which cascade down the Mont-aux-Sources for nearly 1,500 metres. Overleaf: (right) the Caledon River gorge and (left) the luscious land of Witsieshoek, with the Drakensberg on the horizon. In 1969 this area was named Qwa-Qwa when it became the autonomous homeland of the 'Sotho people of the south' or the baSotho ba Borwa.

Bloemfontein (previous page left) is the capital of the Orange Free State and the judicial capital of South Africa. It is a spacious, well-planned city with a collection of fine, classical-style buildings as well as inventive, modern architecture, such as that of the University of the Orange Free State (previous page right). These pages: Kimberley, 'the diamond city', grew up around a hole in the ground, 'the big hole' (below), which is the remains of the Old Kimberley Mine and the largest man-made excavation in the world. Diamonds were found there in the late 1800s and a boom town was born. Out of the chaos emerged Cecil Rhodes, who helped to impose order on the proceedings and founded De Beers Consolidated Mines Ltd. (right, bottom right, and overleaf), an organization which came to monopolise the world's diamond market.

Previous pages left: farming land near Warrenton, which developed as a major vegetable producer when demand from Kimberley increased with the diamond boom. In 1933 work began on a scheme to irrigate the valleys of the Vaal and Harts Rivers. It was then the world's second largest irrigation scheme and was first conceived by Cecil Rhodes. When completed, it transformed the hitherto dry land around Jan Kempdorp (previous page, right) and Hartswater (these pages).

Previous pages: the terrain of the northern Cape is often dry, dusty and unfriendly, yet its sheer vastness can be exciting. Miles of flat sand, speckled with thorny acacia trees, are unbroken but for the occasional, isolated farm, where livestock (right) seems surprisingly healthy, despite the harsh conditions. Facing page: a farmhouse in the arid land near Kuruman (above), enjoys patches of lush, green lawn. Southwest of Kuruman, the workings of the Sishen Iron Ore Mine (overleaf pages) transform the land into a mass of colour, ranging from gentle mauves to the fiery red of iron ore deposits.

The Kalahari Gemsbok National Park (these pages) is unique in that its more than one million hectares consist mainly of semi-desert. However, it proves to be more fascinating than it may sound, for roaming across the wilderness are large herds of magnificent game. Springbok, blue wildebeest, eland, lion, cheetah and many more species seem to live well off this dry land, particularly the splendid, hardy gemsbok.

Previous pages: landscape around Kuruman, which is an attractive town famous for its 'Eye of Kuruman'. This fountain of crystal-clear water is the source of the Kuruman River and provides over 18 million litres of fresh water a day. It was here that Robert Moffat established a mission station that was so effective it became known as Africa's fountain of Christianity. The station also provided a base for intrepid explorers such as David Livingstone. These pages and overleaf: the Kalahari Gemsbok National Park.

Near Upington, the dazzling patchwork pattern of cultivated land in the Orange River Valley (these pages) provides a lively contrast to the colourless aridity of the semi-desert on either side. This lush valley, irrigated by the lower reaches of the Orange River (above), yields a bounty of crops such as cotton, peaches and grapes for the local wine. Its main town, Upington (overleaf pages) is situated on the north bank of the river and is a pleasant and interesting place to stay. It has modern amenities, a fine library and museum, beautiful sunsets and one of the longest palm avenues in the world.

Previous pages, left: from Upington one can visit the breathtaking Augrabies Falls, one of the world's great waterfalls. The name is taken from a local tribal word 'Aukoerebis', meaning 'the place of the big noise'. The torrent reaches its peak during the flood, when over 400 million litres of water from the Orange River plunge into the awesome, 240-metre-deep gorge, creating a thunderous rumble that can be heard for miles around. Also in the area are the huge salt pans (previous pages, right), which produce salt from the Kalahari. Above: the little town of Vredendal, which is surrounded by vineyards and orchards. Facing page: farmland on the Bokkeveld plateau.

Doring Bay (below and left) and Strandfontein (bottom left) are just two of the many beauty spots on the Namaqualand coast. Another is Lambert's Bay (bottom right), home of a large fishing fleet and the haunt of many fine birds such as the flamingo (facing page). Closer to Cape Town is Swartland, where the scenery ranges from the ruggedness of Cape Columbine (overleaf left) to Saldhanha's calm waters (overleaf right), which are rich in rock-lobster.

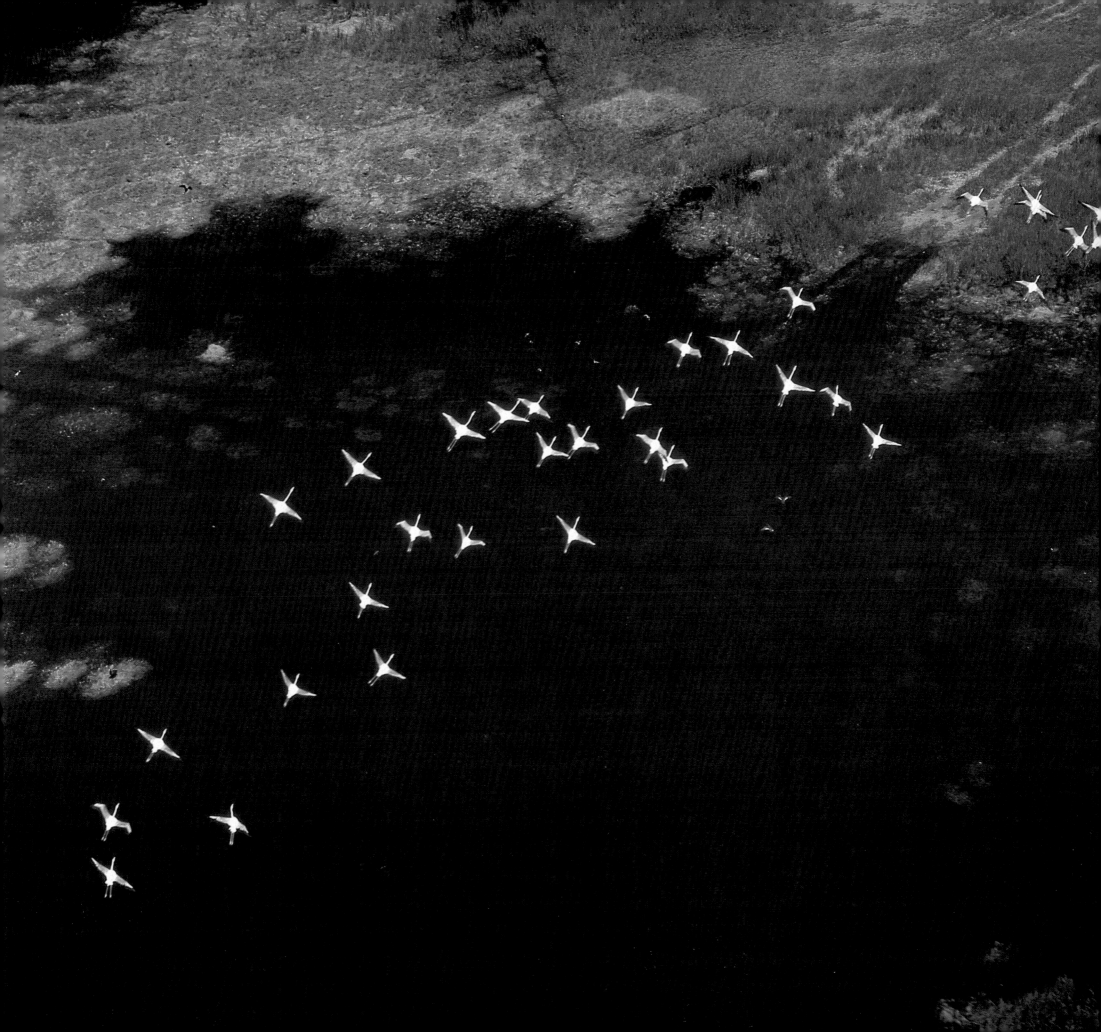